Real Wyrd
A Modern Shaman's Roots in the Middle World

S. Kelley Harrell

Soul Intent Arts
Fuquay Varina, North Carolina USA

Also by S. Kelley Harrell, from Soul Intent Arts

Gift of the Dreamtime – Awakening to the Divinity of Trauma

Gift of the Dreamtime Reader's Companion

By Kelley, from Soul Rocks Books

Teen Spirit Guide to Modern Shamanism – A Beginner's Map Charting an Ancient Path

Real Wyrd – A Modern Shaman's Roots in the Middle World
by S. Kelley Harrell
© 2012

Cover Photo by Jaroslaw Grudzinski
Cover Design by S. Kelley Harrell

Published by Soul Intent Arts, LLC,
Fuquay Varina, NC 27526 US
info@soulintentarts.com
www.soulintentarts.com

ISBN 978-0-9860165-3-0
First printing September 2012
Printed in the United States of America
A Soul Intent Arts Publication

This book is available in print and as an ebook. Visit kelleyharrell.com to learn more about Kelley's writing and work.

Dedication

To all the adults who as youth
saw them,
heard them,
talked with them,
those whom no one believed,
and talk with them
still.

Acknowledgements

Thank you, Live Journal flist, for being my sounding board of reality and wyrd for the last 10 years. You, my literal digital Dream Team, read these accounts when they weren't stories, just my daily life unfolding, twisting. In the wake of shinier, more instantly gratifying social media, our rapport has maintained, and I appreciate your ongoing support and brilliance, most of all your confidence.

Thanks to the readers of *Intentional Insights.* Because of your inquiries and interests in the modern spiritual path, my open dialogue with souls has become a thriving online collective presence.

Always, thanks to Rob, Maya and Tristan, for being the sun, moon, and stars dancing in my world.

S. Kelley Harrell

Table of Contents

Real Preface

For years, on my blog *Intentional Insights*, as Samhain approached with the onset of the Dead Time, I published accounts of my more charged, and in some cases creepy, spiritual pursuits. The Dead Time is a treasured journey to Solstice, thus from darkness to light. As it is a time of untime, the shadowed season presents a great opportunity to tell the stories that many who do shamanic work won't tell--the occasions when things don't go so well, when intuition is trumped by expectation, when the unseen presents itself unexpectedly or in emotionally challenging ways. In the spirit of the Dead Time, I present these stories in the collected body of *Real Wyrd*.

As a lifelong intuitive and shaman by choice for two decades, not all of my experiences with the spirit world have had clear-cut direction, instruction, or even results. Every one of them, though, has meaning. It's not my way to dabble in the supernatural for only the sake of stirring the mystical pot. For me working with the unseen of the earthly realm is an opportunity to learn about life out of form, and be of some kind of service to spirits in need. Working with the other side of death equips me better this side of life.

The Dead Time

To our Western European Pagan forebearers, Samhain marked the beginning of the Dead Time. At harvest's end when the sunlight was in short supply, it was a natural time of thanksgiving. On a practical level, it was appropriate to cull what must be stored for sustenance during winter, what must be seed for the next planting season. Spiritually, it was the time of honoring the spirit world—deities, Nature spirits, and the recently deceased. Closing the year, along with celebrations of successful harvest, so were the dead honored. A place-setting was laid at the celebratory table for those who had died that year, and food was left for them. I would imagine that ages ago, when resources were scarce, the gratitude expressed for the dead at year's end was heartfelt and sincere, as was the enjoyment of the celebratory feast. These were the last decadent celebrations of the year, heralding the bleak winter ahead.

Samhain is commonly called The Witches' New Year, though it was taught to me as marking only the year's end. The new year doen't begin until several weeks later, at Winter Solstice. Just as harvest closed the year in autumn, the return of sunlight at Solstice brought hope for the new year, as well as affirmed survival of the harsh cold. The time between these holy observations was the Dead Time, a space outside mundane time and perception, the mystical birth of the notion that the veil between worlds thins.

The darkest time of the year, the Dead Time brought the depths of winter, from which there was no assurance of spring. Not only was physical survival of the dark winter a challenge, it also tested sanity and stamina.

Worry that there wouldn't be enough to get to spring pervaded life, thus, spiritual observation.

We don't approach Samhain or The Dead Time the same our ancestors. We don't generally live in fear that the light won't return (although it's something to think about), that we won't be fed, or that we won't have the opportunity to manifest our desires. We do however, acknowledge Seasonal Affective Disorder, a cyclic form of depression that many experience in winter, while other socially and economically beleaguered spirits cope with the holiday blues. In light of these modern trends, The Dead Time is still a naturally provocative passage.

As time, itself, seems to suspend between Samhain and Winter Solstice, giving us natural pause to hibernate and reflect on what we're finished with and can leave behind, what we most want to carry forward and grow, we can still experience death and rebirth as our elders did. Hold these observations in mind as you approach the next waning of the sun and the procession to the Dead Time. Enjoy the solitude of shadow, and know the light will soon warm!

What's "Real Wyrd?"

Wyrd is slang, now generally used to describe what lies outside the common perception. I like it. Its original meaning was more along the lines of "personal destiny," with the animistic understanding that All Things are connected. Thus, we're not in a vacuum. Our personal destinies are somewhat intertwined and we affect each other. That all souls affect each other is wyrd.

With that in mind, it seemed natural to call this book *Real Wyrd*. Our culture is quite fascinated with manufactured weird that treats the supernatural as an isolated and separate experience from that of the mundane. I want to present how I experience wyrd as inseparable from all of Life, how that observation has informed my personal journey.

This manuscript is a compilation of true spirit stories that could easily be considered part of the pop-culture paranormal genre. I wouldn't have exactly heralded the unseen into the mainstream quite the way that reality TV and quasi-investigative studies have, though I'm glad such interests have roused contemporary awareness.

Given that, I don't carry around equipment that sounds an alarm when a spirit is near. I don't make notes of the temperature of the room or when I get tingles along my skin (Well, OK, sometimes I do!). I just go through my day and these sorts of things happen.

I'm also not concerned with proving my experiences to others. For me, the proof is in how I find meaning in such interactions, how I allow them to change my life. Recognizing the connection to All Things even in creepy moments keeps me true to my animistic perspective. Finding growth from them is my choice.

The Middle World

To shed shamanic light on how I perceive my experiences with what others would call "ghosts" or "hauntings," consider perception of cosmology. While my personal observation of How Things Are includes many worlds, the commonly recognized terminology of Upper, Middle, and Lower Worlds is easiest to convey.

In this triple cosmology, the Upper World tends to be the place of angelic spirit guides, intuitive healing, and philosophical peacemaking, while the Lower World is generally the space of totems, physical and emotional healing, and earth magick. There are no hard and fast rules around these strata, though giving them some distinction allows the human psyche to connect with and process them. These planes do not appear or necessarily function the same way for every shaman.

In shamanistic lingo, the spirit encounters I share in this book occur in the Middle World, or the unseen of the earthly realm. It is the space in which we encounter "souls with unfinished business;" have strange experiences with natural phenomena (hear animals speak, hear disembodied voices, see orbs, encounter faeries); meet extraterrestrial or subterrestrial beings and angels; feel cold or hot spots in rooms; experience emotions when touching certain objects; find loved ones that have not passed on. The range of experiences that can be had in the Middle World is limitless.

In the Middle World we most readily experience phenomena we can't explain, or that challenges the boundaries of our belief system. For many modern shamans it is the least traveled spirit territory, though for many indigenous shamans, it's prime stomping ground to work with plant and animal spirits, Nature devas, elementals. I chalk this cultural distinction up in part to the fact that most modern shamans simply aren't trained in the spiritual layer of Nature and our immediate surroundings, and culturally, we have been programmed to believe that this strata is bad, evil, and corrupt.

My experiences with spirits began in the Middle World at a very young age, and I honor those early lessons as roots in shamanism. I imagine such is true for many mystics—some odd event on the outer edges of formed being brought awareness of other worlds beyond. Still, most modern teachings shy away from earthly spirit exchanges and don't encourage them. Such interactions tend to be more cast as "dark" or "bad," leaving the Middle World largely unexplored, thus, unhealed.

I suspect that as we are more emotionally involved with this realm than the others, we can't disengage as easily and de-personalize our experiences in it. This is very challenging information to hold for many people, and not to be taken lightly. With that in mind, it can be very challenging to traverse this spiritual plane.

So What?

In this era of insta-psychic and seasoned supernatural guru, we don't find many of our New Age personalities or paranormal investigators discussing experiences that fall outside of their framework or understanding, or just flat out scared the pants off of them. Rarely do you read the viewpoint of an intuitive admitting fear or flaw, personal chaos, or flat out disaster. I promise it happens.

I don't claim to be a specialist in the world of woo. I'm a work in progress, at best, and in that setting that I present this collection of true stories of my experience of the paranormal. In some of them I knew how to respond and bridge, and in some I didn't. Some are light and uplifting, while others deeply affected me and caused me personal distress. It's important to talk about fringe-of-the-fringe experiences, not just to show the humanity of intuitives, but to show humanity the commonness of intuition.

I'm aware that the paranormal investigation genre is being consumed whole by the populace right now, which for people who walk between is a sort of an alternate reality on its own. We're not used to our life view being mainstream. What's widely presented as true paranormal in television and film now still doesn't really chronicle how it is for an *intuitive* who perceives these things ongoing, who has to find emotional grounding amidst these things, and who, frankly, must still function as a regular individual on a daily basis.

It's very easy to poke holes in the conjecture of investigative paranormal TV shows and writings—which I sometimes do. The truth is, people from all walks of life have inexplicable experiences all the time. I've had people from around the world—nonbelievers, believers, Christians, Pagans, aetheists share with me stories of the paranormal that defied not just their beliefs, but their truths. The addition of that scientific observation of the spiritual seems to have the opposite of its desired effect, which is to prove the validity of the unseen. Often the fumbling of instruments and computer data only serves to make such encounters seem more remote, less available.

As well, it's taboo for an intuitive to give up her process. It's a secret. There's little documentation on what the mystic feels, thinks, and experiences while she engages other worlds—and that's not for no reason. The less there is conveyed about the process the more seers can rest in an elitist, esoteric shroud of knowing *oh so* much more. The less we talk about how we came to do what we do, the more it will seem like a special skill that only certain people have.

The thing is, no one has dibs on intuition or the unseen. We all have access to ability, availability. How we choose to work with it, refine it, or even ignore it, is up to us.

What those experiences are and what they mean is also open to interpretation, and most certainly is in the eye of the boo-holder. Working with clients in my shamanic practice has shown me that mystical experiences are far more common than we imagine, we just don't openly talk about them. It's not part of our cultural development to hone them.

Furthermore, I don't really understand "paranormal." To me it's just "normal," and always has been. And what "veil?" I've never observed a separation between this world and any other. They are all conjoined. Generally speaking, once I can distance from my emotional involvement with spiritual phenomena, the experiences, themselves, are pretty... hum-drum. In other words, they're a big, "So what?" Engaging spirits isn't an elitist ability or industry, it's being active in the connection with All Things. It's innate to us all.

About Kelley and the Stories

One of the earliest intuitive abilities I recognized in myself was the ability to interact with the dead. As a child I was terrified of them. They woke me from sleep, made noises in my room, touched me, gave me visions. Nothing in my belief system had taught me that such was possible, let alone how to communicate with them. I didn't understand their symbolic language of acting out the stories of their deaths. I didn't even really know what death was.

As an adolescent I realized not all spirits were products of a completed life in form. Some were spirits of trees, living animals, or beings that have never been in form, who nonetheless influenced the lives of those of us in bodies. Through years of willing that communication to my needs and boundaries, it became a solid method of mutual communication, for the most part.

I am a lifelong intuitive, having focused my work into my intertribal shamanic practice *Soul Intent Arts* since 2000. I am author of *Gift of the Dreamtime: Awakening to the Divinity of Trauma*, the *Gift of the Dreamtime Reader's Companion,* and I am vigorously involved with the worlds in and around me. My work focuses on helping budding intuitives experiencing spiritual emergency (when the soul evolves more intensely and quickly than the psyche can manage) to assimilate their gifts and find balance between their mundane and magickal lives, through the *Tribe of the Modern Mystic.*

When I first incorporated these Middle World stories into my blog, I focused on the scarier ones, because I thought those were the ones readers would be most interested in. I learned quickly, though, that to place such a spectrum of frightful vs affirming on these experiences wasn't just incorrect, it was incomplete. In all honesty, even the profoundly sweet brushes with the unseen are a little unnerving, as the most jarring encounters are also enlightening. In the end, bless the darkness, hold the light, because the two aren't divisible.

Some of these stories you will recognize from *Intentional Insights*, as for several years I shared a selection of them as part of my Samhain celebration. Revised editions of those stories, along with never-before-published updates to them, and several recent encounters are compiled in *Real Wyrd – A Modern Shaman's Roots in the Middle World.*

Whether due to fright or fun, it is worth noting that the most visited and searched page on my blog remains *Hotel Phillips and Murderous Insomnia*, well above all others.

There are many spiritual books on communicating with the dead and discarnate, though most of them only extol the wonder and awe of that work. They don't talk about the toll it takes on personal lives, or the emotional perils faced learning to be healthy conduits for spirits. Indeed this work is wonderful and awesome, but it can also be scary, disorienting, and uprooting. I share these accounts of paranormal exploration as part investigation, part curiosity, and part luck of the draw in being a human equally aware of her soul.

In the end, there are many factors in how we connect with spirits and process things we can't explain. State of mind, as well as perception of ourselves and Life shapes what those experiences are and what they mean to us. What we believe spirit visitors to be influences how they affect our lives. What we believe ourselves to be dictates how we react to them.

    Dream well.

    ~skh

    October 2012

Chapter One - Hotel Phillips and Murderous Insomnia

In early spring of 2002, I had the fortune of spending a week at the beautiful Hotel Phillips in Kansas City, Missouri, while on a business trip.

I'm quite used to loads of spirit traffic when I stay in hotels; however, my stay at Hotel Phillips offered a bit more than the luxury experience the lush establishment touts. From the first night that I checked into Room 1513, I sensed many presences–again, not unusual at all, as I do quite a bit of psychopomp work. Staying in hotels for me is like being tapped on the shoulder constantly, far from restful, and Hotel Phillips was no different. Upon checking into their rooms, other people hang up their clothes first thing, spread their toiletries, find area restaurants. I create sacred space and release errant energies, a gesture part compassion and part hopeful of a solid night's sleep.

On this occasion, one presence in particular stood out right away—a female whose only visual aspect was a white lace hem that I saw close to the floor. I saw "her" in my room and hall several times the first few days that I was there, though she wouldn't allow me to feel her etheric field. What was odd about this spirit was when I offered to release her she didn't want to go. From time-to-time spirits aren't ready to leave for any number of reasons, and I left her to herself. Primarily focused on the work that brought me to the city, I just honored her distance and let things go. I also got a sense with this presence more than any of the other errant ones that passed through that she had indeed died in the building, and needed friendly company. Regardless, I couldn't sleep in the room. She wasn't particularly bothersome or ever-present, but her air of unrest was contagious.

Two mornings into my stay, I got up, showered, and was drying my hair in the bathroom when I felt that I wasn't alone. The feminine presence was in the room.

I opened the bathroom door to find a distraught woman standing at the threshold. She was about twenty-two to twenty-five years old with long auburn curly hair, a Caucasian woman in a rather formal 1930s style drop-waist dress. Her white hem fell just above her ankles—the garment I had been seeing all week. As I gazed upward, a large bloody wound in her chest dripped blood and tissue onto the floor. She'd been shot in the back and was experiencing the panic of her death moment before me.

Seemingly in shock, she wouldn't budge from the doorway. I stepped out of the bathroom and through her, as she moved to the side of my bed. I didn't learn her name, though she was cloaked in a strong sense of betrayal. It seemed she had become involved with a man and the relationship couldn't, for whatever reason, come to fruition. This man shot her.

When spirits visit I often learn information around the cause of death, and it's always fascinating. I'm tempted to delve into their stories and learn about their lives and deaths. Yet, staying true to my role as psychopomp means that such details are mere curiosities. They aren't the work, itself. For me to prod into their personal straits would be like a doctor stretching a wound, rather than stitching it closed. Thus, the only real objective with the dead is in learning how I can facilitate helping them move to the next phase of their destiny, then doing just that. Everything else is superfluous. That said, sometimes learning what I must to help them shift before they can move on is no easy feat.

I asked her if she wanted to be released, and she hesitated. I told her that she wouldn't have fully shown herself to me if she didn't want help, and I asked what held her here.

My sense was that she was waiting for the man who killed her—her lover—to somehow redeem himself. Often the dead don't move on due to some third party objective that I don't have access to. I can only work with what I know, and knowing nothing about the circumstances of her relationship or death, I stayed focused on how to help her. I told her that she may have a long wait, that she'd already had a long wait, and that she could wait for him to make amends in a much better place than this lonely hotel. After a bit more discussion, she allowed me to walk her into Spirit space and all was restful.

I finished readying myself for work and went on to my teaching session. When I returned that night, from the minute I entered the room, I was uneasy. The oppressive stuffiness of the room was worse than when I first arrived, and the gloomy presence was angry at me. I knew it wasn't the woman, yet the spirit refused to communicate.

Once in bed, the lights were out for about two minutes when a low scuffling came from a corner of the room—like a large rodent in a paper bag. The sound grew extremely loud and I began to hear it in different parts of the room. Rooting in the walls, under the bed, the sounds grew louder.

I lay listening for a few seconds, when finally the crescendo behind my headboard formed a complete circle around the bed. The entity meant to frighten, if not threaten me. This intention became more evident when the discordant sound resonated with pressure on my body, a firm weight crushing on my ribs.

I'd been rattled by all the theatric noise and movement, but non-consensual physical contact from spirits is an extremely disturbing phenomenon. For me, when an encounter reaches that point, fear becomes anger, and I was pissed.

Enraged, I sat up in the bed and observed a male in the room, about four feet from the foot of my bed. Although well-dressed and clearly well-to-do, he was surrounded by black clouds. He appeared Caucasian, though physically didn't appear entirely human. His life force was exaggerated beyond a mere human, though it was clear to me that he was of the earthly realm. I knew this man was the woman's killer, and that he had killed many times. He was a nasty piece of work, and he was angry at me for interacting with the woman.

He had killed her in the hotel (assuming it was a hotel at that time), though not in that room, and he'd never been linked to the crime. His pride was wounded that I knew what he'd done, as he was used to getting away with everything. Having seen his dirty deeds, he wanted to eliminate me as a threat. He was afraid that I would hand him over to some authority for punishment. He was so stuck in a defensive consciousness and his personal drama that he didn't realize that he was dead.

I told him that I didn't care what he'd done in his life, that I wasn't there to judge him. He didn't believe me, though as I continuously said the words his energy gradually softened. The noise in the room stopped. I told him this wasn't the place he needed to be anymore, that whatever happened between him and the woman was between them, and if he felt ready to deal with that from a more useful space that I could help him get there. I also made it perfectly clear that I was ready to sleep and we would not be negotiating all night.

At that, the clouds around him began to dissipate, but I still didn't see him clearly. I held the space to release him for a good forty-five minutes or so, but he went relatively easily, thoroughly. For the first time since I checked into Hotel Phillips my room was quiet on all fronts.

The next morning I approached the concierge, asking if anyone had reported anything strange about Room 1513. He, along with the staff at the front desk, went pale and asked me what had happened. When I told them that I saw a woman in my room, they stammered a bit, eventually going on to say that they hadn't had reports about *that* room, and no disturbances had been reported at all since the hotel had re-opened post-renovations that fall.

They offered to assign me to a different room, and when I declined, they huddled in the corner whispering. Clearly they were aware of creepy occurrences, but I couldn't tell if they would be relieved or disappointed to learn that their gangster spectre and his damsel were no longer guests.

Chapter Two - A Sprite and a Bullseye

Not exactly 'bump in the night,' this experience creeped me out as much as affirmed. The afternoon of note was mid-week, sometime in the Fall of 2003.

On my way from work one afternoon, I stopped to return an item at a popular mega-retail store. Frankly I was in a really bad mood, annoyed to have to make the return, and doubly perturbed to be doing so at the end of my work day. To boot, the line was very long and not budging. I was extremely self-absorbed, my inner talk consisting mostly of complaints and expletives. I was oblivious to my surroundings, save the woman who was waiting the line in front of me.

I couldn't tell much about her, only that she hunched over the push bar of a shopping cart, one foot propped on its lower rung. I thought there was a little person in the cart's seat, as the woman murmured softly. Every few minutes a matchbox car would fly from the general area of the cart. The woman would retrieve the toy, then resume her slumped position until the car flew out again. For whatever reason, I didn't perceive anyone in the cart.

The process of retrieving the toy repeated a couple more times, but all I registered was how the line had not moved. I was tired, my feet hurt, and I just wanted to go home. I couldn't have been more wrapped up in myself or my annoyance. We stood there a few more minutes, when I heard a little voice say, "Kelley..."

I froze. I hear my name called out all the time clairaudiently. This time, I registered immediately that it wasn't a spirit voice calling on my personal frequency. Someone around me had said my name.

Looking around, I saw no one I knew, certainly no one who should know my name. An odd tingling sensation rippled through my energy and I stepped out of line to peer around the woman leaning on the cart.

Indeed there was someone there. Peeking around the woman was one of the most beautiful little boys I've ever seen. He was maybe two years old and looked back at me with dark, coffee eyes. Bubbling with fae-like enthusiasm, he gazed straight at me and said, "Kelley! Hi!" His speech was plain as day, his smile bright and huge, as was the light all around him. The little boy truly was hard to look directly at for the brilliant glow around him.

I've always been good at feeling etheric fields, and this kid was on a different channel, spiritually speaking. That was immediately obvious about him. The woman, whom I presume was his mother, turned to me red-faced and spoke something I didn't understand, clearly shushing the giggling child.

What I didn't understand in her words, her life force said loud and clear: This wasn't the first time he'd done such, and it embarrassed, if not frightened her. She hurriedly quieted him, but I could tell the little boy was mischievously aware of what he'd done and he wouldn't be silenced.

I don't know why, but my eyes started watering, and I said "Hi" back with a little wave. He giggled more and his mother nodded but didn't make eye contact with me. She approached the counter as the line finally moved.

I stood shocked. Completely gobsmacked and keenly aware of my surroundings, no one else in the line seemed to have registered a thing. Why would they? Planes of being hadn't shifted and opened up to them, affirming that the link with All That Is is always at work, slicing incisively through foul moods in return lines.

I found myself having an internal conversation with this little boy over the next few minutes, thanking him for letting me know he was there, that he cared enough about my mood to risk speaking to me in a very special way, and for showing me something very dear about himself.

I thanked my guiding spirits for letting me know that not only are there more of us out there, all ages and varieties, but for telling me that we're living on multiple planes and having very different experiences, without shame or hesitation, even in national retail shopping chains.

Chapter Three - Charitable Neighbor

This episode occurred in the mid 2000s, on a cul-de-sac in North Carolina's own super suburbia, Cary.

Feeling the death experience of another Being is not an odd occurrence to me. The sensation of my body's systems shutting down, the pressure of hands wringing my throat, the aching chill of life draining from a fatal wound—all are rather familiar. Not to say that all deaths are so dramatic. Some are quite gentle in passing.

Growing up, feeling others' deaths were my most frightening spirit encounters. I didn't understand that these beings meant no harm (for the most part), but were seeking acknowledgement, compassion, help in transitioning. The only way they could communicate with me was through sharing— or demonstrating—their stories.

As an adult I rely on the help of my spirit guides to help me experience others' deaths and maintain my wits while helping invading spirits move on. There have been cases in which souls tell the story of their demise with my body but don't want to move on and that's when the efforts of my guides are most needed.

Most of the time now, I experience the deaths of others only within dedicated psychopomp rituals. However, it seems the most common time for me to experience spontaneous death moments of the clingy variety is in the wee hours, between 3-4am.

Though I am accustomed to feeling my body be some soul's last attempt at biological life, I found myself very disturbed by this specific soul that just couldn't let its number be up.

A cultivated level of higher awareness kicks in during these dark hour death experiences, and it was within that altered framework that I knew instantly that I wasn't the only one in my body. When I realized something was wrong, my awareness was addled. I was aware that I lay in my bed, that it was dark outside, and that I was convulsing. My heartbeat was scant, my lungs labored for the smallest puff of breath, and my limbs were leaden. I registered that the sensations were exactly that—*sensations*—and not mine. Once that realization of perspective kicked in, I emotionally detached from my feelings and could react.

I called in my guides, who scrambled in and around me, in what I call 'cosmic triage,' doing whatever it is that they do to hold the boundaries of me in place while sweeping the extra life force out. I attempted to speak with them, and at no response decided to just observe and wait it out patiently.

The whole ordeal lasted probably maybe four minutes, and when my pulse finally regulated and my body calmed, I sat up and took a few deep breaths. I'd just begun to ground and recoup lost rest when the bed began to shake. Looking over, my partner lightly convulsed. I've mentioned before that I'm willing to walk a long line of allowance in the work that I do, but when it turns to real threat I get very angry and that's always when things get interesting. The spirit had been evicted from me, but had hopped into my lover.

Immediately I called in the directions and began to track the spirit. As soon as I specifically located it in my partner's form it leapt from his body and vanished, though I could still sense it around our house. As my partner lay still and breathing smoothly, I projected myself through our entire property looking for the transient life force.

I started in the attic beams and worked my way through every room, cabinet and closet, even the gaps around the appliances. When I found nothing I walked the perimeter of our yard, then crawled through the mailbox to no avail. I could feel that the spirit was still there, but I couldn't track it. It was dodging me completely. Then it occurred to me then that I hadn't checked the chimney.

Diving down the maroon brick length, I found nothing and came to light in the living room facing the fireplace. As I stood with my back to the room pondering my next move, I realized I wasn't alone. Movement shifted the back of my hair. Something was touching me, then a very large body pressed against my full length, from behind.

In a split second I broke out in chills from head to toe, and turned to see a transparent, enormous creature projecting partially into my physical space. The being was sort of human, but not entirely.

Masculine, the creature was easily eight feet tall and four feet wide standing upright, though he had small horns on his head and what may have been tusks. He felt very old, primordial, even, and seemed to draw on anger and human/Nature disconnection deep in the land. Energetically, the life force reeked of everything dysfunctional and offensive, and I was immediately repulsed. Even if this entity hadn't been still trying to attach to me, the predatory aspect of its nature was enough to make it harmful to anyone.

Having felt that oppressive energy, I had a vivid understanding of why my guides worked so furiously to move this entity from my form. He had a very fond connection to darker aspects of human nature, and he wasn't ready for that part of his borrowed biological experience to be over. He'd no intention of going quietly. In fact, he had no intention of going at all. I was appalled that after having tracked him and experienced his disposition, the Being was still trying to crawl into my form.

Thoroughly disgusted, I told it point blank that it couldn't stay in my house and I entertained no dissent on the instruction. The Being didn't want to move into Source space. I coerced it as far as the divide between our house and the neighbors', but couldn't budge it from our property. I knew I couldn't force it the rest of the way, and I couldn't just block it out of our etheric space. The Being was revolting and I couldn't just abandon it to turn up on the neighbors' doorstep. I called in my guides to deal with it the rest of the way, then watched, trembling, from my vantage point in our bed while my spirit teachers lifted the wayward spirit.

No sooner had I returned fully to my body and opened my eyes than all around our cul-de-sac home security alarms went off in tandem. Over the din my partner sat bolt upright in bed and asked me what had happened. All he recalled was having a bad dream, though as I recounted the series of events he nodded. He'd felt something in his body earlier, then the convulsing, only he'd thought it part of the dream. Then, as we settled back to bed the screeching siren of an emergency vehicle pierced the night, its flashing lights coming to a stop at a house in the cul-de-sac behind ours. My partner and I looked at each other eyes wide.

I don't know what happened that night. I don't know if indeed a neighborly host in the other cul-de-sac died, sending its sinister visitor to make house calls in hopes of finding new biological real estate. I know that I'm eternally grateful to be able to do the work that I do, and for the support and wisdom of my spirit teachers.

An addendum to this experience occurred a couple of years later. Having based my shamanic practice in our home, I made regular sweeps of errant energy to keep the domestic and etheric bliss as balanced with the land elders and Nature spirits as possible. While that singular entity had moved on, I repeatedly found vestiges of similar murky life force in that house and surrounding land, even up to a few miles from our little cul-de-sac. I dutifully hosted *mesa blancas* to clear the area, and each time we did, an angry land spirit would emerge and refuse to leave.

Talking with a friend and fellow energy worker one day, I mentioned this to her—that no matter what depth of work I did alone or in conjunction with other healers, I never felt like the land there cleared, which was one of the factors in our decision to move from that area. My friend's expression went peculiar as I spoke, then she told me an interesting story.

I didn't grow up in that area, though as a North Carolina native, I passed through it many times going west, before it became the super suburbia that it is now. I can vividly recall the woods and bee supers edging the fenced yards of white-frame houses that dotted meadows surrounding Hemlock Bluffs and what is now a major shopping development nearby. My friend not only remembered the area that way also, but she knew the woman who had owned a huge tract of that land.

She said that about twenty-five years prior, the old woman who owned the land had been conned by the developer of that shopping center. Health failing at the time of the sale, the woman's relinquishing of the land rested contingent on one demand: that the developer not take down the beautiful pine and oak trees that dotted the land.

Of course the young man had no intention of honoring that agreement, and he razed the soil bare of every growing thing. When the old woman saw what he'd done, she cursed the land, and she told him that the shopping center would never prosper.

That's all well and good. Who doesn't love an 'old-woman-done-wrong gets her comeuppance' story? But it doesn't end there. I watched that shopping center come in with the first ultra-modern theatre, mega-gym, multi-leveled fountains, up-scale restaurants, spas, parking deck. This shopping development was the prototype of the current mini cities sprawling every suburbia, now. It was the area's preeminent one-stop entertainment facility. There was nothing like it in the Triangle Area at the time. And one-by-one, every shop that went in it failed. No one could figure out why. By every estimation, that development was the cutting edge effort of the town's commercial offerings. It certainly made no sense to me that relatively nothing could sustain there, and what did was by a slim margin.

My friend went on to tell me that around the same time that I was focusing releasing work on the life force I'd found in the area, a relative of the woman who had cursed the land came to her and told her what had happened. Desperate to turn a profit, the now mature developer asked the family member to release the curse. The old woman had died years ago, and her remaining family didn't know how to undo it.

They asked my friend to go to the shopping area and lift the curse.

The family member and my friend completed a ritual to release the curse, as well as to heal the rift that the construction caused between humans and the land elders and Nature spirits. Within a year the development was under contract with a construction company and began renovations.

Just this year it re-opened with a few stores—none of which are the original retail features. In addition to new spas, fancy eateries, and high-end markets built into the hill's natural slope is a water fountain, which winds through the center of the plaza, a playground, and lots and lots of trees.

Was my ghastly night visitor connected to the events at the shopping center? My feeling is that my guy was causing trouble in the area well before that shopping center broke ground, but conjoined anger fueled both rifts. What was evident to me in the two stories, though, was that the land was speaking its hurt, and each in our own way, we heard it and responded. Whatever led to the anger and breakdown between humans and Nature, after giving the land attention, all was quiet.

Chapter Four - House on Summit Drive

At this point I hope it's obvious that words like "ghost" and "haunted" don't come up in my vocabulary. I've learned that those words conjure charged reactions in people, implying fixed ideas about spirit activity. My unusual education in soulful arts has taught me that spirits deserve to be put in categories as much as people, and every case of otherwise unexplained activity should be examined unto itself. It's become very hard for me to call a suffering spirit, a mischievous faerie, a hyper-polarized piece of land, or the projections of a deeply troubled consciousness a "ghost." To me, we are all spirits, interconnected life force.

Of course I didn't always make those distinctions. When I look back to my childhood, I recall having interactions with spirits pre- kindergarten. At that age and until my mid-teens, neither my culture, my upbringing, nor my emotional maturity allowed me to view those experiences as anything other than the traditional model we are given for ghosts. I filtered all those interactions through lenses of fear, trauma, alienation, and victimization. In recounting those experiences now it is my goal to present them as they were to me then: scary.

I lived with my mother, my older sister, and two collies for most of my youth, and we all witnessed some pretty disturbing events in the house where I grew up. We lived on Summit Drive, in Goldsboro. The most recurrent of these events usually happened at night, and that was the sound of a man's heavily booted feet coming down our hardwood hallway, stopping right at the juncture of our three rooms. We never had trepidation about the presence, itself, but the shock of hearing those thudding footsteps never abated.

Another frequent collective event involved our clock radios. Each of us had a clock radio in our room, and it was a regular pastime for all three of them to turn on at the same exact second in the middle of the night. No other electrical appliances or timepieces in the house were affected, but playing with clock radio alarms was popular with our visitor. Again, no real terror involved, but the element of surprise never lost its edge.

While not as frequent but loads more frightening, several times we awakened to what sounded like all the silverware being shaken inside the kitchen drawers, only to find not a thing out of place upon examination. Along that line, we woke on at least one occasion by what sounded like every window in the front of the house being smashed out, though found nothing harmed.

Those very repetitive events were flat out unnerving, though there were isolated encounters. On rarer occasions the upright piano played by itself while it was closed, just a few tinkling notes. (I had that same piano until a few years ago, and on occasion it still played itself, closed.) A favorite prank to play on me, in particular, was opening the kitchen cabinets. I could walk out of the kitchen and return later, knowing there was no one else in the house, and find all of the cabinets wide open.

It's also relevant to add that the two dogs we had were always on guard when these things would happen. One of them reacted defensively to our bumps in the night, while the other cowered and couldn't be coaxed into areas where something odd had recently happened.

These were events that we all at some point witnessed. My sister and I each had some harrowing experiences alone in that house, too. One morning when my sister was twelve to thirteen years old, she sat waiting on our front porch for the school bus to come. My mother and I were already gone. While sitting on the front step, she heard a rap on the window behind her. Knowing that she was the last one to leave the house, and having locked the door herself, she became afraid. Looking back over her shoulder she saw nothing in the window, though the curtains fell back into place, as if there had been someone there holding them open.

Years later, just after my sister was newly licensed to drive she came home to an empty house late one evening. Entering through the dark kitchen, she stood near the sink when slow, heavy footsteps sounded from the far end of the hall moving toward her. Pulling a knife from a nearby drawer, she froze and the footsteps stopped. There was no one else in the house. Knowing that my mother would be home shortly, she waited outside in the dark, feeling safer there than in the house.

In my younger years my mother put me to bed early so that she and my sister could enjoy the close of the day together. One particular night, I lay drowsily in bed, listening to their chit chat and spoons clinking in mugs of tea. I remember lying on my back on the bottom bunk of my captain's corner beds staring fixedly at the ceiling, tuning out all but what they were saying. After all, what kind of little sister was I if I missed anything?

I stared upward, straining to hear what they said. I recall my vision cutting out for a split second, though I still heard them, then I felt myself lifted three or four feet off the bed. The pressure of arms scooping me up constricted my ribs so much they hurt. I draped in them, suspended for a few seconds, then was flipped completely over and flung rather unceremoniously face down on my bed. I hit the bed so hard it moved on the hardwood floor and I smashed my forehead into the headboard. I started screaming immediately, "That wasn't funny! You scared the crap out of me!"

Of course they both came running, and my mother frantically switched on the light. I babbled on about what had happened, blaming them, and my mother assured me that neither she nor my sister left the kitchen, let alone came to my room until they heard me scream.

I listened to my mother talk, but I remember looking around the lit room reasoning that I had been lifted to a height higher than my top bunk. I also recall leveling with myself that neither she nor my sister could have picked me up, let alone thrown my body any distance. The bruise on my forehead the next morning indicated that someone could, and apparently had, as I also had faint red marks on my ribs. This was the only time I recall ever feeling physically threatened by the dynamic in our home, and that fear stayed with me for a long time.

Through my early teens, I had slumber parties for my birthday. The year I turned ten several girls slept over. We'd had an evening of pizza, cake and silly television, then retired to my bedroom to gossip behind a closed door and listen to music.

My mother, long since gone to bed, yelled at us every few minutes to turn the record player down. We would turn it down, then slowly work back up to a dull roar. We sat on the floor jamming, when we heard heavy footsteps pound down the hallway, then stop right outside my bedroom door.

All of my friends knew that odd things happened at our house, but the house spirit rarely acted up when we had guests. We sat there listening to a light scuffle just on the other side of the door as my mother yelled at us for running down the hall. I recall listening to the muffled ruckus and throwing the door open, to find nothing there. I don't think my mother enjoyed having a bunch of screaming little girls to soothe, but it made for a memorable party.

When I was around fourteen years old, I went through a particularly difficult time. I recall one evening after an altercation with my mother, I was very upset. I curled up in bed and cried for a quite a while when I felt someone sit down on the bed behind me. The mattress dip toward my fetal form, and I instinctively shifted back against the form that pressed into mine. A cool hand swept back the hair that stuck to my damp cheek.

I lay there for a minute or two considering that I was still angry at my mother, yet feeling I should address her given her nurturing gestures. Raising up, I started speaking to her and turned to look behind me, only to find there was no one there. I was the only person on the bed, though for a few seconds the cool touch lingered on my cheek and I could still see the dip in the mattress. Gradually the mattress raised back to an uncompressed state and I knew my comforting visitor was gone.

Another night when I was about sixteen years old, I woke for no particular reason to find a man and woman standing to the right of my bed, a woman at the foot of my bed, and two figures to my left. They were all dressed in black, and they stood slightly above me looking down to where I lay. The man was holding an open book in his hands, and was reading from it. I could see his mouth moving though I heard no sound. Their style of dressed was turn of the 20th century long dresses, bonnets, stiff tailored suits. I had the distinct impression I was crashing a funeral, and I had the vantage point of the corpse. The odd thing is when I jumped at seeing them, they stopped their ritual, gave me a shocked look, then vanished.

Years later I spoke with our neighbors about the odd events in our house. To my surprised they'd had their own. They, too, had every radio and alarm clock turn on all at once repeatedly in the wee hours, and they'd heard heavy footfalls down their hallways. One guy a little older than me said he'd even looked up at one point to see the matchbox cars he'd lined neatly on his desk plunge one by one to the floor.

I don't think about the events on Summit Drive terribly much, now, odd as that may seem. I register with detachment that they were frightening, yet they were also somewhat routine for us. I've also lived in a lot of different places and know now that every space has its unique spirits, imprints, and phenomena. I do wonder, though, if the current owners of the house where I grew up have the same spirit guests.

Chapter Five - Higher Consciousness Shopping

Apparently the American trend of vast strip malls is a bad idea, energetically speaking, as it seems I often have bad experiences in them. I'm fairly sure I'm not the only one affected by all that hyper-focused energy. This event in particular happened in the winter of 2006.

On my way home from work one day I went to the newest, shiniest Walmart in Raleigh. The whole mega-center area on which it sits is very discordant for me and I don't go there often at all. As it was, a specific item that I needed was only at that location, so off I went.

From the second I passed through the enormous automated doors something was wrong. My temple literally twinged, some synapse torqued strangely, the tingly effect of it rippling through my body and etheric field. I truly should have turned around and left immediately but my consumerist hunter-gatherer instincts would have none of it. Once inside, the fluorescent patina bore down and I hesitated to get my navigational bearings. When I did, I noticed something very odd: it sounded like a radio was on, inside my head.

I am quite clairaudient so I didn't pay a lot of attention to the buzz at first. As I made my way through the store, I realized that when I passed directly by certain people, the buzz would clarify into distinct words and phrases. As I passed by different people, the voices changed.

I passed a young couple and two voices went through my head at once, lovebirds individually cooing over each other. Then I passed a woman and heard a proliferation of expletives about having to find a specific item for someone else. It wasn't until I passed a little girl of about six or seven years old holding the hand of an old man, that I realized what was going on. I heard her little voice begging for someone to get her away from the mean man, and I realized I was hearing peoples' thoughts. I was spontaneously, though unintentionally, cosmically eavesdropping.

I recognized the phenomenon for what it because it happens almost every night when I lie down to sleep. In hypnagogic states most people see abstract visuals—conversational blurbs, distorted light or random scenes, until they shift into sleep. For those who are aware, this state is the precursor to lucid dreaming. I do sometimes see odd visuals in pre-sleep but most of the time I flip through the bandwidth of the Multiverse, hearing anonymous conversations, voices, music. It quite literally sounds like a radio dial skimming stations, never quite settling on one for any length of time, though the phrases that manage to come through are distinct. Sometimes I hear several conversations and languages before I fall to sleep. This bedtime ritual I gave in to early in my childhood, and I never really think about it too much.

However, standing in the middle of Walmart I couldn't think of anything. My head was full of everyone else. I had never felt anything like it before, and frankly I never had reason to consider it possible. As soon as I processed that the little girl was experiencing deep distress about the man with her, I began to project back to her, telling her that she was powerful and she could overcome anything that she needed to. I didn't know what else to do. I couldn't walk up and accuse the man. I couldn't readily engage the little girl.

Silently, I told her that I was with her and loads of angels and lightbeings walked with her, and that we would all do our best to take care of her. I felt sick at that point. I didn't want to hear anything else. I forewent the object of my trip and started to make my way out of the store.

As soon as I stepped out of the door there was an audible crackling in my head and I had an instant migraine. It hurt so badly that I was in disbelief that I wasn't bleeding from my ears. I hadn't had a migraine in a few years, and never had one so suddenly. My head hurt all the way home, and I still heard voices as I drove.

When I got home I lay down, with everything spinning inside me and out. I tracked the pain to a specific spot in my head and in it I felt a rapid exchange of information—the cosmic equivalent of some

Multiversal mainframe. It wasn't harmful, per se, but the physical pain, itself, came from the furious exchange of data. I asked my guides to come in and facilitate as gently as possible whatever was going on in my brain, and in about forty-five minutes the headache was gone, and I was the only one in my head.

I maintain that the ground beneath that shopping center houses some kind of hyper-charged grid that's not getting along with the super suburbia atop it. I don't know what alignment of elements triggered the event in the store—timing, aliens, dental work, planets... I have no idea.

Personally, I like to think I was upgraded.

Chapter Six - All in a Day's Work

For sixteen years I've worked as a technical writer for a state agency housed in the renovated old Rex Hospital in Raleigh. The hospital, itself, was functional in the mid 1930s through the late 1970s, becoming my agency in the early 1980s.

When I first came to work at the complex I didn't know that it had been a hospital, though the greeting of trauma energy as soon as I entered the building was a profound clue.

My tension was confirmed within my first hour there when I was told that it had been the largest hospital in the area, at its inception. Shortly after I received my ritual office hazing with the 'ghost stories' of the spirit nurse in Elevator 1 who likes to play with the buttons and skip floors, the murmuring crowd that can be heard when alone in the building, doors opening and closing on their own—the usual paranormal fare. Of course accompanying those stories were ones of the collectively marked infant graves in the courtyard, various rumors about blood in the morgue (though I never saw that), and just general mumblings of uneasiness in certain areas of the complex from a grounds keeper.

Intent on my technical writing gig, I left the woowoo at home. I showed up everyday, did my work, and called it a day. I never had any intention of mixing business with... well, business. Of course it wasn't long before I started having odd experiences.

It started out innocuously enough, hearing my name yelled out in an empty room (I had a huge office to myself for about a year), hearing the door to my office open and shut followed by the footsteps of someone walking up behind me, though no one would be there when I turned around, and an ever persistent feeling that someone was standing behind me while I was working. Events reached a crescendo when I felt an unseen hand linger on my shoulder one afternoon.

I've set the intention fairly clearly that I will allow spontaneous spirit communication because that is part of my job as a deathwalker. However, I'm not receptive to being randomly touched by any stranger, living or spirit. After feeling the hand on my shoulder, I completed what I needed to do for the day then went to my car.

In the parking lot, I held space for the dead to move though for half an hour. They came in droves. I'd never experienced a mass psychopomp event before. They never stopped coming. The only reason that I ended the session was because I was tired and it was dark outside. I felt bad for the truncated session, but I had to respect my own boundaries. Nobody wants a tired deathwalker.

I sat with the memory of that session for a long time, and as a result became more tolerant of the spirit interactions of my day job. I no longer separated my jobs. Part of my arrival routine became to greet the dead much as the living when we pass in the hall—which, by the way—on several occasions I've passed random people in the hall, brushed right up against them, only to glance immediately back to find no one in the corridor but myself. It has truly become the norm. When I softened to the regularity of spirit visitors they began to interact with me more, particularly after my office was relocated to the 4th floor.

I don't know what the 4th floor was used for in the hospital, but as soon as I moved up there I began to see a few spirit regulars. One in particular was a young African American woman in her early teens standing to the far left of the sinks. She was dressed in a very simple peach colored shift with a tiny hat the same color. She wore white gloves and clutched a white pocketbook tightly in both hands, at her chest. She gazed at the floor, and didn't seem happy.

Uninterested in talking with me, she silently conveyed that she wasn't a patient at the hospital. She had been a loved one of someone who had died there, whom she hadn't gotten to visit. The understanding that her loved one was no longer in the building didn't occur to her, but she was afraid to be released. I didn't coerce her to leave and went on my way. I saw her several times, always in that same spot, and we always greeted each other amicably.

One afternoon I was sitting at my desk when I felt her come into the office. Her mood had brightened considerably and she wanted to be released. I don't know what readied her to go, but she passed easily on to Source when another soul came. I held the space for that one to move through, when more continued to come.

I sat for maybe fifteen minutes as spirits moved through. However, even with all the movement I observed something unusual. There were hundreds of them observing the parade of souls, some even venturing to come up very close to my face, as if I was an oddity to them. In that session I felt that these were not all souls of those who had affiliation with the hospital. In fact, some of the souls I was sensing had never been human at all. Some had never even been in form, but were discarnate wafting entities.

When I closed my eyes and visualized the campus from above, it appeared as a vast vortex extending deep into the ground with thousands of souls meandering in it. Energetically, it was a stagnant thread in the web of the whole area, when it should have been a free-flowing Grand Central Station of souls, easily sliding Here and There. Despite the number of souls I sensed in the space, those seeking to pass through had dwindled. Many were lingering just to watch.

Having spirits converge at a focal point then not facilitating some kind of release for them isn't the smartest idea, but it's also futile to try to force one to move on when it doesn't want to, let alone to try to force hundreds. Yet I felt that this stagnancy was happening for a reason and I needed to honor it even if I didn't understand it. I had my guides call on the guardians of the land there, to create the safest most supportive atmosphere possible for all souls inhabiting the space—living or discarnate. I figured if I couldn't move them through, the default was to make the space comfortable for us all. I checked on the situation fairly regularly, though, holding brief sessions to release those who were ready.

That was more than five years ago, now, and I continue to work with the space. No matter how many sessions I hold at the old hospital campus, souls never stop coming to pass through my openings for them. I have come to regard the campus as a haven for souls who indeed have endured some sort of trauma, even if that trauma was only not passing peacefully into What Comes After. I've also concluded that there is something about the land, itself, that attracts all of these souls. What was built on it in modern times as place to care for others was merely focusing the land's innate power to do just that. Perhaps with time and attention the land will give up more of its mysteries.

Chapter Seven - Number One Rule of House Selling

In early 1999 my partner and I decided it was time to purchase our first home together. We looked primarily in the Raleigh and Cary areas with the aid of our wonderful realtor. One Saturday in particular our realtor scheduled us to visit more houses than I could have ever imagined possible in the span of about three hours. Little did I know how overwhelming that would be for an intuitive!

Going into any unfamiliar space is a bit harsh on the senses for an intuitive, but going into many in a short span of time nears overkill. I'd not had the intimate experience of unabashedly walking through someone else's personal space without that person present, and that dynamic of energetic intrusion was equally as discombobulating as feeling so many strange, new spaces.

We went into a couple of houses that felt peculiar, though for no specific spiritual reason. When a structure feels uncomfortable, the assumption is often made that there is a spiritual presence causing the unrest. Though there likely are spirits on every square inch of the planet doesn't discredit such factors as elemental influences, electrical charges, ley lines, random anomalies of physics that we can't readily account for, etc, as influences over how we feel in a space. For this and other reasons we've seen the rise of Feng Shui in the western world as a refined art in creating harmonious living, elementally. My unrest in most of these houses seemed to be just that— born of them not being the right balance for us.

We entered one house in particular, in Cary, that felt a bit odd. There was no alarming sensation, nothing I could put my finger on. It was a nice little split level, though not quite what we are looking for. My lover, realtor, and I meandered through the house, eventually going our separate ways. I explored the upper level while my partner was in the lower level, the realtor in the mid-level.

As I was checking out the upper guest bathroom, a woman in a dark dress walked past the door. Thinking nothing of it, I finished my solo tour then came down the stairs. I paused at the mid-level, taking in the vantage point of the center of the house. I glanced back up the stairs, and saw a woman in a black dress with fine white polka dots step from the hall into the very back bedroom. I marveled over the dress, as it was a rather full skirt, the sort one used to see floating atop a petticoat in 1950s style dresses. In the previous homes we'd viewed, other realtors were in and out with clients. Aside from the odd style of dress, I didn't really give more thought to this woman being in the house.

After a few minutes we re-convened at the mid-level when the realtor said we could go ahead out and she would lock up behind us. I asked her why she needed to lock up when there was someone else in the house. She looked at me like I was clearly ill and said that there wasn't anyone else in the house. I told her what I had seen, and being the dutiful realtor she charged up the stairs to sleuth out the stranger.

My partner and I looked at each other, shrugging. I genuinely thought there was someone else in the house—I had no reason to think otherwise. I had my feelers on to check out the unseen aspects of the house and had no ill feelings about it at all. The house felt quite light.

The realtor came back downstairs insisting that there was no one in the house, and by that point I believed her. She looked at me like I was completely nuts and brushed past me to open the front door. As she and my partner were walking out of the house I glanced down into the lower level where a toddler—a little boy—in a walker stood stock still just at the bottom of the stairs. He chewed a pacifier in his mouth and looked back at me. I don't recall any particular communication between us, just the mutual acknowledgement that we could behold each other. The realtor called to me again and we left.

We decided against that house on practical grounds, though I wasn't thrilled with the thought of moving into a place so energetically cluttered that the spirits were already making contact, even if they were benevolent. The house that we ended up buying was also in Cary (yes, *that* house), and it was cosmically frenetic, though in a different way. It's no wonder looking back that I stayed worn out when we lived there.

Generally speaking, the town has a quartz bluff that runs through part of it, which in my estimation accounts for a lot of its chaotic vibes. Because of the quartz veining, the area is known for having an inordinate amount of lightning strikes. Our home was about four miles from that core. That combined with the restless state of the land influenced my work greatly.

Before we moved into the house, I began journeying to the house and land, allowing both to know me and to get a feel for how we would all merge into the space of Home. From my early journeys to the Nature spirits on the property to the very last ones working with the general land before we moved from it, I had the constant feeling that the land in that area struggled with some ancient interdimensional wound, which only exacerbated any human-related spiritual unrest, of which there was plenty.

When we first moved in, the most frequent visitor was the wife of the previous owner. She was living; however, the couple had divorced and some facet of her soul didn't want to give up the house. I often would walk into the kitchen and find her standing defiantly in front of the stove. After a few talks she was willing to concede my kitchen and I released her to Source.

Moving house is a huge energetic transition. Some land functions like static electricity for emotions, thus holds imprints of events, creates vacuums for spirits. Some structures hold so many great memories they can't help but be places that discarnates want to linger. And much as we wouldn't leave behind our entertainment center or the dog, so should we be aware of not leaving behind aspects of ourselves.

Strange as it may seem, sometimes it's not spirits of the dead peering from the windows of deserted houses, but spirits of the living. Go into spaces with the attitude that what needs to be released can be, that what facilitates compassionate living stays, roots. Whether coming or going, do the healthy thing for all involved and declutter.

Chapter Eight - Angel Download

The year 2007 was rather strange for me, for several reasons, largely because two vastly significant segments of my life intertwined. In that timeframe health conditions that I'd managed through an intense spiritual emergency came to a head (Chapter Eleven - Saturn's Gift), as well as I began to have mindful interactions with Star People, whom I suspect are also the Light Choir many speak of—uber high "angels," for lack of a better description.

I'd read stories of experiences in which people had stellar visitors who affected their neural functioning, in essence 'changing their hardware' to ready them for emerging frequencies coming into the planet. I'd never felt myself as part of that strata of experience. I was a shaman, an earth-dweller, a Nature spirit in my own right. I'd had many experiences journeying out into the starry vast Unknown, but I had not experienced that facet of the Unknown venturing to me.

Many of my colleagues communicate with that level of Intelligent Light, reporting such physical sensations of ringing in the ears or a cool droplet of water over the third eye as indicators that such a communiqué was occurring. I had no reason to think that I would engage in that facet of spirit communication, and that was fine. Truth told I always found it somewhat hokey, talking with angels and aliens. By most measures I've had my hands full unraveling the myriad experiences of the wryd throughout my *mundane life, I didn't need to court something extra.*

In the fall of 2006 I began to have migraines. I'd not had them since 1999, the time I now look on as the beginning of the second most critical spiritual emergency in my life. What made this episode of discomfort different was that my face went almost completely numb on the left side, I suddenly couldn't hear well, and had problems reading. All sound seemed to be at a great distance and under water, tinged with a persistent low ringing. Visually, it was as if I'd suddenly become dyslexic, only it wasn't just that letters and words inverted on a page. I began seeing symbols that were unrecognizable along with upside down letters and blank spaces mid-sentence.

With the rapid onset of all of these symptoms I returned to the neurologist I'd seen years before. Medical exams yielded that nothing had changed or was harmful in my brain. The neurologist tried to convince me that I'd always been dyslexic but at the age of thirty-five just "hadn't noticed" until the present.

Being the sort who knew she wanted to be a writer at the age of five and set her entire scholastic agenda to that outcome, I knew this was a new development and that I hadn't been latently dyslexic. My sense was that something major was going on etherically, a very profound shifting of synaptic wiring, so to speak. Medically, no diagnosis was reached.

Headaches persisted over the next few months and I began to have a very difficult time articulating myself. The visual phenomenon abated for the most part, but my hearing was still quite affected. I consulted my spirit guides ongoing, and they informed me that my etheric form was shifting at a rate far more rapid than my physical form could comfortably withstand. As well, they told me that I was clearing out chakral clutter, which was resulting in various chakras elevating into vastly different vibrations than I was used to overall, and that other chakras were feeling very uncomfortable as they hadn't reached that same point of or need for elevation yet.

While I felt my guides' assessment to be fact and I found peace in that confidence, I was physically miserable. I began having headaches more severely and sought out a fresh perspective on my neurological landscape.

In early March of 2007 I went to a different neurologist who also held a rather holistic practice as an osteopath. She immediately confirmed that I'd not suddenly become dyslexic, but that indeed a cerebral event had occurred. From her perspective it was imperative to assess just what that event was. From my perspective, I wanted to see how the body's mapping was changing to suit my new etheric territory. I consented to the testing that she wanted to do, which initially included another MRI.

The results of this MRI were different than the one I'd had six months prior, revealing scaring on the brain as the cause, according to my doctor, of the physical symptoms I was having. In order to rule out deeper implications for the cause of the scaring she ordered more tests.

About a week later I was cruising down Raleigh's outer beltline when in a flash, electricity rippled through, not just my body but the whole car and space around it. In that instant, I saw a group of lanky silvery-grey Beings standing in a walled space surrounded by huge boxy electrical conductors. Though their life force somewhat blended into a collective, they felt predominantly feminine, and they looked back at me through the windshield the way one looks at animals through glass in a zoo.

As soon as the Beings realized that I could see them they gasped and appeared rather sheepish, imparting a very clear sense of playfulness at being caught with a hand in the cosmic cookie jar. In another blink, before me was only highway. I heard the murmur of a collective voice say, "She knows we just pushed this down." I heard other voices, but they were hypnagogic, fluid, not unlike ambient melody. I heard this soft strain the rest of the way home.

The intensity and pervasiveness of this experience was very much like my strange mind-reading experience at Walmart, only the data coming in this time was purely pleasant. As I drove along, bemused, the meaning of this exchange was perfectly clear. I've read many instances in archaic history and modern experience of Star Beings collectively injecting radical transformation to passively open up options to an energetically stagnant populace. I never had cause to disbelieve it but I'd never experienced such, personally. This intervention had been personal in that I felt it, but it also stretched beyond me over the land, in the space between the Earth and the firmament. It wasn't totally personal and yet was custom fitted to every Being who could receive it in this plane.

For all the strange encounters that I've read about, this one that took place in the car I saw happen. An image actually opened in my mind that didn't originate from me, and I knew it was a radical transition being gifted the population instantly. The entire event lasted about six seconds. I felt surrounded by a silvery aura that wasn't my own afterward, like an etheric cushion to keep me from hurting myself with my new information, a buffer to assimilate. I laughed the rest of the way home. I realized then, that my wyrd had moved up to an entirely new level.

Medically, my doctor performed a lumbar puncture to discern the origin of the scaring on my brain. The results of this were normal, though an unrelated but peculiar outcome was the revelation that I apparently tend to be lower than the norm on spinal fluid, which can create a collection of annoyances, none of them particularly threatening. I walked away from the physical observation of the changes in my body knowing that my brain had indeed been remapped, a cause for concern to my neurologist, though to me it was a mirror of what I knew to be happening in the shifting template of my life force.

The last event in that sequence of changes came almost ten days later. In the early hours of sunlight I lucidly became aware of existing in two spaces at once. I lay in my bed, though I was also lying in what appeared to be an encampment in another plane. The scenery was a small arrangement of beige tents and bedding flanked by tall waving grasses of a meadow. There was a rather bleak feel to the space, though, as if it was a temporary meeting place between realms, a multiplanar MASH unit.

I lay on a beige pallet on the ground, surrounded by about 20-30 others reclining nearby. They, too were consciously aware of their location and of being outside their bodies. I recognized one of the people as a childhood playmate, someone I'd not seen in years. A Being stood over me, fairly masculine in energy, and quite a large presence. He reached into my head, specifically into the area of my brain that bore the scars. I felt him moving things around, and I became extremely agitated. I fought him with all the energy I could muster, all the while having an inner dialogue with my spirit guides. They told me that it was his job to "install" the etheric component of the changes that had been made in my physiology and that it was up to me to decide if I wanted to allow it.

"Will the headaches stop if I allow this?" I asked.

They informed me that gradually they would abate with this new balance of energy.

"What will it change in me?"

As soon as I formed the thought, the Being plunged its "chip" into my brain. A jolt of electricity shot through my body and crackled far out into my etheric form. My ego was quite distressed about this gruff handling, though I knew that having uttered my last question I was expressing positive intent. By the time the energy traveled several feet out into my form I felt marvelous. I noticed an indescribable cellular rapport, as if I was finally able to experience all of myself in a basic formed manifestation.

Indeed my neurological symptoms did calm significantly after the culmination of this series of events. I began to see silvery white orbs on a daily basis that I know to be the consciousness of creatures guiding us into a much wider practice of experiencing ourselves in this plane.

Chapter Nine - Faeries in the Garden

I'm not a skeptic by any stretch, but I am an experiential junkie. I need some level of personal exchange with a phenomenon before I can fully give myself over to its reality, even if that exchange happens purely in the ether. I've realized that there can be a wide berth between knowing something is entirely possible and experiencing it to be so. I've also learned that when experiencing something energetically overlaps witnessing it physically, such an opportunity is a gift.

Several years ago I was attending a weekend class at the retreat Terra Nova Center, in the mountains of North Carolina when I saw faeries. The location, itself, is somewhat of an anomaly in that it sits at the convergence of several ley lines. I personally believe it sits between diverging strata of time and dimension based on other intriguing experiences I've had there, but perhaps that's more of a personal gnosis.

The caretaker of the retreat has a very close relationship with the faeries of the land. I'd visited the retreat several times and heard stories from the horse's mouth of the fae striking a deal with the caretaker, in that if she would tend their portal on her land they would commune with humans—by invitation only—between Mother's Day and Summer Solstice each year.

The caretaker told us how through general conversation with them she learned what their job was in this realm and how they did it. They told her that their purpose was to collect dew to protect the sacred seed within blossoming floral life, which apparently they take very seriously. They let her know that they enjoy colorful, shiny trinkets. In an attempt to better understand their work and forge unity with them she complimented them on the plants and overall landscape. They replied, "That's gnomes. We only do flowers."

The night I met them was the evening after Summer Solstice of 2002. It was the close of the faeries' interactive season, as well as the pinnacle of what had been months of dreadful drought. The caretaker told us that the fae had not been very active at all through the summer, as they had been struggling to maintain the flowers.

In agreement with the caretaker our class met in the faeries' garden around 9:30 that evening. There were only a few of us, maybe ten to twelve, and we were told that upon entering the garden people often feel the sensation of a cool droplet on their forehead, or have ringing in their ears.

I felt nothing of the sort. I remember crossing the threshold of the garden and instantly feeling as though I wasn't supposed to be there, as if my presence was an interference. I had the distinct impression that my tension was an indication that the presence of humans, at least at that taxing time in their season, was pulling the faeries' energy in the wrong direction. My feeling was that we shouldn't focus so much on them appearing to us, as we should just let them tend their jobs caring for the garden.

I sat in the talking box, the bench the caretaker usually perched on when she conversed with the fae, waiting for something to happen. Group members wandered peacefully about in the lovely open space. Eventually, I meandered to a level area toward the front of the garden that overlooked a flowering planting bed at the base of the mountain that rose just behind it. To one end of that bed stood an old chimney, the portal, of which the caretaker said the fae called "the tower" that allowed them to pass from their world to ours.

I'd reached a point of blissful meditation on the mountain and wasn't even thinking of faeries when one of the women who worked at the retreat grabbed my arm and exclaimed, "There she is!"

I all but jumped out of my skin, jolted from my peaceful state, but when I looked in the direction she pointed, sure enough there was a brilliant blue spark wafting through the dark night. It glided down the mountain and came to exactly where the lady had dragged me. Mere inches from my body, the light circled my midsection. It regarded me as a stranger, as much as I curiously observed it. The blue spark drifted amongst the group, weaving between all of our bodies, squeezing between tree limbs, rising above our heads and sweeping past our feet.

The whole time I there was chatter in my head, ticking off the things the flying light could be. I wasn't intentionally trying to disprove what was right in front of me; rather, it was more like a reflex of my mind reinforcing *that* it was right in front of me and I had no context to suit it.

The spark was bigger than a fire fly and it stayed lit for long intervals. Even when the spark would dim a halo of blue stayed lit several inches out around it. Each of us stood in awe, even the retreat worker who'd seen them many times, watching the blue light greet us. About the time that I gave over to the idea that I had no idea what I was witnessing something even more strange happened.

A few smaller golden sparks lighted amongst us, but the slightly larger blue one flashed into a big orb. It literally exploded into a blue ball of light as big as my hand, the bright spark at its center growing stronger with luminous force. The spark in the center continued to float out amongst us, dimming and lighting while the glowing ball around it remained consistently lit.

I know what I saw visually, and it fits into no other phenomena I can source. Etherically, I observed a profoundly peaceful stratum of Earth's experience of itself that required nothing of me but to honor it. There aren't many better ways to spend a weekend.

Chapter Ten - An Afternoon With Max

A phenomena well-known to the mystical community made widely popular by the film "Indiana Jones and the Kingdom of the Crystal Skull" is that of ancient skulls honed from precious and semi-precious gemstones. Found scattered throughout Central America and Mexico, a particular set of thirteen crystal skulls thought to be the ancient relics of tribal mystics have been interpreted many ways. Some say they are connected to the Mayans and will serve a cosmic uniting purpose at the end of the Long Count in 2012. Some say they are metaphors for holographic consciousness, devices for divination and higher awareness. Others say that they were hand-delivered from space beings for some collective purpose yet undetermined. The conjecture is endless. What is known is that these gems are between 5,000 and 36,000 years old, most are carved from a single crystal block (a feat modern technology has yet to reproduce), that they are priceless, and that my partner and I did a session with one in 2003.

I first read about the crystal skulls a few years earlier in *The Mystery of the Crystal Skulls: Unlocking the Secrets of the Past, Present, and Future,* by Chris Morton and Ceri Louise Thomas, a book that I selected out of mere curiosity and interest in crystals. *Max, the Crystal Skull,* as it is known—one of **the** crystal skulls—is in the possession of JoAnn Parks of Texas, and is from time-to-time made available for private readings and sessions. When I learned that Max would be visiting the Triangle Area I leapt at the opportunity to do a private session.

Our instructions from the host were short, but specific. No touching Max, and stay in the seats provided. It seemed simple enough.

We entered the shrouded room to find Max displayed rather dramatically on a lighted pedestal. With only an hour for our session, we promptly sat in the metal chairs lined up before the skull.

I stared intently at the vacant, sightless sockets. In seconds an intense migraine seared through my left temple. Daringly, I touched Max and my palms warmed, tingling lightly after I withdrew them. I focused on relaxing, altering my breathing pattern. Calling in my guides and whatever aspects of Max that would want to communicate, I slid into a light trance.

Poised with paper and pen, waiting for something amazing to happen, I began to hear a male voice. It told me to sit with both feet flat on the floor and to press my palms together in prayer position. When I did, for the first time since a car crash two years prior I felt no pain or discomfort in my body. At the time, I couldn't remember when my body felt so at ease.

I sat in trance a few more minutes, enjoying the comfort of my body, when a creature stood up out of the skull. It appeared as a naked Austrlian aboriginal man whose body was completely covered in a white powdery substance with hints of silver and dark blue mixed in. Small leaves the size of an ivy leaf grew from his flesh, and they, too, were the powdery white. He danced in front of us, then danced in a circle around us, silently. His energy was of an elemental, though not one that I recognized. Energetically, he felt the same age as Max.

After about 20-30 minutes of playing congregation, I abandoned the proffered char and lay on the floor a few feet away from Max. Trance facilitation is best for me when lying, so I assumed my usual pose. As soon as I was flat on the floor, the voice started yammering in rapid-fire stream of conscious. I hadn't time to set an intention or direct the interaction in any way; it started instantly. Ever the scribe I stopped trying to listen to Max and wrote as fast as I could.

What it is and where it came from I do not know. The purpose of Max and its cohorts remains a mystery. In the spirit of honoring that ancient puzzle I share an excerpt of its words to me:

> *Kelley, take heed in your own guidance, your own council—the world is small and your space in it large. This love knows. This love grows. Understand that your role in exactness is simple—live. Live in everything that you do. Do not be hindered by the trivial ties, for you are bound to nothing. There is*

*nothing you cannot do. You will write
this all. You have written it all.*

*Please hear your own voice in what
you say. You have chosen it, the tool,
the words. It is uncommon such
devotion. Never doubt this. You are
dear. Let your body free its chains to
stricture and common. You know its
rivers' sanctity and holding are deep
with fervor.*

Chapter Eleven - Saturn's Gift

Saturn. The name of the mythical Roman god elicits shudders from historians and astrology enthusiasts, alike. The wielder of justice, the task master, the great leveler of the playing field... Likewise, Saturn—the planet—is all business. With the intention of forcing you to face what you have not, this stellar body moves into a new sign about every three years.

Practically speaking, this means that it occupies the exact location in the natal chart once, roughly every 28-30 years. Saturn Returns, as such are known, are surrounded by much hype largely because they bring three years of intense personal clearing and transition. Considered a cosmic vice that will bear down on what you have not prior been able to release or move, rumor was that after all the intense purging managed by Saturn, the impartial judge would leave his tenderized charge a gift. Little did I know how hard I would work for that gift, or what that gift would be.

For me the fun began in March of 2001, with a car accident that left me in extreme pain for about three years and health conditions to manage ever after. That first year, I had intense kundalini explosions commonly referred to as a spiritual emergency. That was my first Saturn Return. Immediately after that came Saturn taking up station in my sun sign, which is not a common synchronous event. Where most people have the approximate three years' liaison with Saturn, I had six. The first three years were a profitable time during which I wrote and published *Gift of the Dreamtime*, inadvertently bringing me a great deal of healing. Willing to accept that as my gift at the close of my Return, I elected to follow Saturn's lead for the next three years.

In July of 2005 I was staying alone in a hotel when I became aware of a presence in the room. I had already cleared the room, as is my traveling norm, and I was surprised to find a spirit there. When I closed my eyes I saw a spiritual manifestation of my grandfather. He told me that he was leaving and that he wouldn't be back in this realm in form again. It was a peaceful interaction, though I carried no particular sadness at his announced departure. In my childhood he had sexually assaulted me on numerous occasions, the healing of which was thoroughly brought through in my Saturn Return. The next day, the day that Saturn left my birth sign in 2005, my grandfather died.

Despite the fact that I wasn't close to him in any loving sense the news hit me fiercely, literally leaving me dizzy and needing to sit. My life force changed on the spot, some primordial thread passed from him to my father, to me. In my lack of grief I remained oddly raw for a long while after, in a way that I couldn't articulate. I felt exposed energetically, and no matter what I did, couldn't regain grounding or protection. Aware of this lack, I focused on connecting with my spiritual allies and left the situation in their hands.

During this time one of my cats, Phoenix, began to act strange. Years before he had made clear to me early in our fifteen-year relationship that he was my familiar. In a conversation I'd asked him what that meant exactly and he said, "I'm your companion."

"What does a companion do?"

"Keep you company," he glibly replied. I didn't ask him anymore questions.

In that timeframe after my grandfather's death I frequently found Phoenix talking with a presence in the guest bathroom. He always sat facing a particular spot, staring at it and caterwauling deep conversation. If I interrupted he would glare at me until I backed from the room, then he would continue talking. I didn't know what was happening but it was clear that Phoenix wasn't alone. As the cat was unfazed by the exchanges, excellent energy judges that cats are, I left him to it. My sense of the dynamic was that Phoenix was orchestrating something and I simply wasn't part of it.

By February of that year we began finding blood in the house--huge crimson sprays on the walls and carpet about 6-8 inches in diameter. At the time we had two cats and a dog, all of whom presented perfect health. Two months later, Phoenix began to show signs of vestibular imbalance, and I was at last with him during a projectile nosebleed. Mystery solved, this condition followed a pattern of him being immobile for days, then he would bounce back to light, life and playful kitty-ness. Evident was the fact that his body was under extreme duress, though his veterinarian found no cause for or proof of his symptoms.

I was keenly dismayed at his odd decline. Having facilitated the deaths of several animal friends, upon talking with Phoenix I expected him to advise me of his life plans and what role I might play in them. To my surprise, he told me to do nothing. He told me that he was finishing work on another plane and that he would tell me when it had been completed. Clear to me was the fact that if I did facilitate his death to alleviate my grief it would be against his wishes.

The pattern of gruesome explosions continued, along with Phoenix' chipper little personality telling me to hold the space for him to complete his work. He began talking to his friend even more. The presence in the house became overbearing and by this point in my grief, my ability to fend off unwanted spiritual influences was almost nonexistent.

Phoenix stopped sleeping at night and wailed nonstop. He ate well, groomed, and kept to his usual routine of napping in the yard and his favorite sunny spots about the house. Frequently I asked him, to his annoyance, if he was ready to die. He told me repeatedly that he was not and that I was, with no ambiguity, *not* to euthanize him unless or until he specifically told me to. He told me that he had work to complete that would be more beneficial to do while he was still in form. According to him, if I euthanized him before that point it would complicate his process radically. Sadly, I left that governance to him and listened closely.

All the while that we supported Phoenix, other strange things began happening in the house. Our dog began to exhibit vestibular imbalance, and lights began to flicker randomly throughout. There came changes in my own health. Within the space of about two weeks the problems with my hearing and vision began, the brain re-mapping, etc.

One morning that August, Phoenix began crying in the wee hours. I gathered him around 3am and we lay on the couch. About an hour later I was awakened by a bright flash that settled into a horizontal sheet of white light cloaking the room.

I sat up and observed that I could see above and below the hovering blanket of light. Phoenix began crying in my arms while the dog and other cat became agitated and left the room. Again there was a blinding flash and one of the computer monitors turned on. Instantly after, the four desktops simultaneously turned off. The room was deadly silent in the absence of the technohum, and a masculine presence became evident. It hit me then that Phoenix had been buffering this energy and that his ability to continue buffering it was declining.

In about two seconds I went from startled to livid. I approached the monitor that had turned on and saw that despite the fact that the desktop was displayed, none of the CPUs were actually on. I switched the monitor off and was enraged.

Realizing that I was too emotionally involved with the situation to affect it I called on a colleague to help. Right off the bat she isolated that my grandfather was clinging to me and was manipulating my lower chakras. She didn't know anything about my past with him, and I was genuinely surprised to hear her assessment. She went on to say that he was intentionally interfering with my sleep cycle to disrupt my usual healing work in my dream state, and that he was specifically dumping his karma on me to avoid having to do the work himself.

My many spiritual interactions with him had always been geared toward my own healing, never to just interact with him. To that end, they were very peaceful, very compassionate, which is largely *why* the healing of my childhood experiences with him could manifest so completely. I was genuinely taken aback to learn that not only had he not transitioned thoroughly, particularly after his visit to me in the hotel the night before he died, but that he was lingering to cause me more harm.

When I told my friend this she informed me that the aspect of him clinging to me now was not the higher, balanced being I'd experienced healing with so many times in journey and the night before his death; rather, it was the earthly consciousness that was deeply troubled and still perpetuating abusive patterns.

Properly armed, I came home, thanked Phoenix for his protective efforts, and cleared the house. I closed those of my grandather's chakras that had remained partially functional after his demise. Three days of persistent entity release rituals transpired before the suffering aspect of his earthly consciousness completely transition. When it did I told Phoenix that he could relax and that he no longer had to do the work alone. His relief was evident, but he told me that his work still wasn't complete.

On 21 November I was admitted to the hospital with appendicitis. While I was waiting for surgery Phoenix came to me and told me that he was ready to move on. I lamented that I couldn't help him and he assured me that there was no rush. He just wanted me to know he was finished.

On 10 December 2006 we went to the vet with Phoenix, though we came home without him. His deathwalk was very difficult for me, yet it became clear in that procession that Phoenix had released me from very old, harmful misogynistic life threads. I also felt that he was paving an opening for radical etheric change in my life and in his own destiny.

At his death I realized just how much over fifteen years Phoenix had contributed to grounding my life force. Physical evidence of that etheric transition came in March of 2007, when my neurologist confirmed that I'd had a series of minor strokes that left several physical markers, countless unseen ones.

What, then, did Saturn gift me?

A deep and lasting release from limiting patterns.

A budding insight into the vast and incomprehensible nature of consciousness.

An opportunity to work through lingering anger toward my grandfather.

An understanding that part of grief is not emotional, but the changing etheric field.

An appreciation for the physical manifestation of widening awareness.

More than any of those Saturn left me thankful for unconditional love and soulful support most evident in a truth of Wise Women lore that says when her familiar leaves, Woman steps into her true power.

Chapter Twelve - What the Spirit Board Said

This little story was quite frightening in hindsight, and for that reason I have not shared it until this publication. Almost two decades ago, I had an experience that taught me why spirit boards shouldn't be used by laypeople as conversation facilitators with the discarnate. Not only am I vehemently against them being marketed as games, but the science of divination is not one to take lightly in any format.

At that point, I was already on my path of intrigue with all things esoteric, and I'd long known that a planchette from a spirit board would stall under my touch. It could be zipping along under tentative other fingers while I observed, but as soon as I felt the cool veneer beneath my own it would halt. Truly, I should have realized then that it was Divine Intervention, but I am not without my blindspots. Plus, my divinatory handicap seemed resolved when I realized that with one friend in particular that little mass-produced messenger would fly. Under her fingers and with my voice, I scribed hours of fascinating other-worldly discourse.

We were at her home one afternoon when we decided it was time for a board session with the spirit that had been bequeathed to her via a family member. I pause to say that she is the only novice I've ever known who could use such a board without harm, and I feel it is solely because this particular spirit had been in communication with her family via similar instruments for two generations. Cultivation of that relationship is what protected her, as well as consistently using a specific opening ritual. My friend always started her sessions enacting a specific pattern, so that she and the heirloom spirit would recognize each other.

Once past the ritual hazing the real interaction began. Her bond with this sprit was so cohesive that 'he' would ask us how we were and offer insight on events that had transpired in our lives since our last session with him. Working with this being was fascinating. Sometimes he shed insight on topics that had come up in conversations we'd had hours before the board was even taken out of the box.

One such occasion my friend and I had been discussing the odd predicament of a friend, then our conversation eased into to other items of interest. Later in the day, we decided to do a session with the board, with no specific intention in mind. No sooner had we the board on the table and the familiar ritual sequence begun, than without any question or provocation, the planchette flew, spelling out the name of the friend we'd expressed concern over earlier, and underscoring our thoughts on the predicament. We'd long since forgotten the conversation but the spirit board hadn't. That it darted about sharing insight in our friend was unnerving, an act which affirmed that even when we're alone, someone is listening. Moreover, this interaction only underscored to me that the relationship with this spirit was and remains a unique dynamic for me in spirit dialogue, with regard to using a board.

We then spent the first few minutes with the planchette circling wildly until her familiar kindred came through. My friend dialogued with the spirit over some personal concerns, seeking insight into life choices she felt unsure of, then we took a short break.

When we came back, questions I had, however, took a different route. I'd been working with my spirit guides and wanted the perspective of her spirit familiar. I asked it to tell me something about my guides. Without pause it indicated that one of my cats was one of my most powerful spirit teachers.

Somewhat sated, we meandered a bit with further questions, general information-gathering about how the spirit world was different than formed being, how all of those differences still enabled us to connect with one another. Just before we were winding to a close I asked her familiar to tell me what I needed to know most at that moment. It's a common request I make of my guides in my spirit visits regardless of vehicle, and again, I wanted to test the waters in this odd medium.

After hesitating, the planchette spelled out the name of a loved one, then "j.a.i.l." Perplexed, I didn't understand what the connection was on an etheric level, as this person had loose connections with law enforcement. It wasn't a revelation that this person would be associated with jail.

Quizzically I came back with an aptly eloquent, "So?"

Part of the lure of such archaic forms of divination lies in the seductive neurology of receiving their message. The question is put out there, nerves crackling, eyes wide. The lull before movement begins baits the senses fully, followed by the zinging sensation in the hand, rhythmically guided around the board, brain struggling to group discordant letters into cohesive words, struggling into the realization of the thoughtform, itself...

The board spelled the same word, nothing more. No matter what clarification I asked for, the board only spelled, "j.a.i.l. j.a.i.l."

We'd never had chilling moments using the board—touching ones certainly, even sentimental ones with this particular spirit. But she and I both looked at each other confused, sputtering that something was horribly wrong with the message. It just didn't feel right at all, or even like it was coming the kindred spirit.

In those few seconds something came over me. I felt smothered, like I was running, choking on too much air coming in too fast. Bitter cold bit at my bones, and I was terrified. A sense of sheer desperation came over me and I thought I was going crazy, certainly paranoid. I felt hunted and desperate, and I didn't understand where the feelings were coming from. Cliché as it seemed, the room had turned cold and the chill moved close, pressing in on us. We decided to call it quits, chalking the discourse up to adverse etheric weather.

I would be lying if I said that the interaction with the board hadn't left me quite rattled. It did, but since I had no context connecting that fear with the facts of the message. I let it go. The information left my conscious thoughts entirely.

Seven or eight years later, when I was culling through journals of Rune readings, autowriting sittings, and our spirit board sessions, I found the notes I'd scribbled from that day. My chest exploded with an anguished ache as I finally made the connection between what the board had said and what I'd felt.

Mere weeks after my friend and I had done that session, the loved one whose name was spelled out got into troublesome scrapes that resulted in... jail time. Upon release and just before trial was set, my loved one was found shot to death in the woods, mid-winter.

I learned two things from that experience. One is that intuitively, I fare better as my own vessel for spirit communication. My guides assure it. The other is that regardless of medium, without that relationship to my guides in place as the filter for information coming in, I'm quite vulnerable.

The moral of the story is that it's not that you can't learn important information

from garden variety spirits in passing, it's
that perhaps you shouldn't.

Chapter Thirteen - An Unearthly Warning

The incidents in this encounter occurred in October of 2011, and only marginally include me. This experience reminded me of the many reasons that spirits visit us and introduced me to a phenomenon I hadn't experienced before.

Earlier this year my sister, Ellen, expressed concern that something odd was happening in her home. Hearing these words I perked up as her house often has interesting, but soothing activity from peaceful spirit visitors. The mountains of North Carolina are very active spiritually and etherically, and she resides at the heart of the region. In fact, we've even ventured to say that the exact spot of her home is a rejuvenating place for souls in and out of form. That something out of the ordinary distressed her gave me pause.

We didn't have another opportunity to talk about what was going on before I went up to her place for a visit. That area is always very "busy," so on general feel alone, nothing registered out of the ordinary to me, which is to say it felt extremely busy. However, as we all wound down for the day and casual conversation came up, something new happened. My nephew mentioned having experienced something odd in the house. My sister has often acknowledged visitors, and my niece has on occasion reported interesting events. This was a first for my nephew.

He began by sharing with me information he hadn't told his mother, which was that one night he'd heard pacing upstairs in the small hall between his room and his sister's, which leads to the balcony that overlooks the living room. He heard individual footsteps shuffling over the hall carpet, the boards supporting the balcony creaking with each step. It went on for quite some time, then eventually stopped. He also indicated hearing a woman's voice along with the footsteps.

At that point my sister chimed into our conversation, saying that was the exact spot that she'd heard someone walking, directly above her bed downstairs. She'd been home alone at the time. Though she'd not heard a voice, she sensed that the presence was feminine. Fairly comfortable with experiencing such phenomena herself, she wasn't at all happy to learn that it was affecting her kids.

As we discussed what spirits are and how to interact with them, I put feelers out around the house. Again, I got nothing beyond the usual busy stream of life force that I know is typical for her home. Things felt peaceful.

A caveat of this story is that since having twins, I've been highly conscientious of sounds that come through the baby monitor. From the first minute that we moved them into their room to sleep alone, I kept an ear tuned to pick up hints of their distress, but also for sounds that did not originate from them. Of course, I'd heard none. However, later that same evening at my sister's, my partner and myself were putting the babies to bed in the third upstairs room. I was highly aware that this was the area where the pacing woman had presented herself, but I trusted my perception. Everything felt fine. The spare room was a bit upended as it was in the midst of being cleared for painting, but it was fine for the babies. We put them down for bed and shut the door behind us.

My partner headed downstairs, and I grabbed the monitor from my nephew's room then turned it on. As I walked down the hall toward the balcony, just in front of the room where the babies settled I heard muttering through the monitor. What instantly struck me as odd was that I could hear the babies chattering through the monitor as well as with my ears, but the muttering only came through the monitor. I froze, and heard nothing. I took a step back, and there it was again. Plain as day, I heard the croaky voice of an old woman muttering. I couldn't make out what she said, but she was distressed, very upset. The other feeling I had was that she had no intention of leaving, that she was protecting something. I attempted to engage her but she didn't respond. I listened to her and my children for about a minute, then the voice stopped. With careful steps, holding the monitor out before me I tried to locate the voice again and could not. It was gone.

I was a little rattled that I'd heard what we had just been discussing moments earlier, and that for the first time I'd experienced Electronic Voice Phenomenon. What really bothered me was that beyond feeling the spirit woman's distress, everything about the home and area still felt peaceful. This observation didn't at all mesh with the intensity of her upset, and it definitely wasn't aligned with her etheric assertion that she wasn't leaving. Posing a completely new dynamic for me, I was confused.

Returning downstairs I described what I'd heard to the rest of the family, and we discussed it further. We all agreed there was nothing malevolent about the visitor, but that she was insistent about being there. Despite my best efforts in trying, it was futile to release her at that point. The old woman would not budge. Taking a different approach, we all discussed what the boundaries were for visitors in their home—those in form and those not—we spoke them to the house and general area, then left it at that. Nothing further happened that weekend.

A few weeks later I got a frantic phone call from my sister. In the process of finishing the third room, she was overcome with a sense of dread. Repeatedly, as they prepped for painting, she verified that the power was shut off to the room prior to removing the outlet covers and light fixtures. Despite being 100% sure that the electricity was off, she was inexplicably terrified.

As they got to the last outlet—the one that was seldom used and shared a wall with the balcony—they discovered the socket, itself, was loose. Upon attempting to tighten it, the socket fell out of the wall and fire shot out. Not only was the socket badly corroded and its wires burned through save a tiny connecting filament, but apparently that outlet was on a totally different breaker than the rest of room. Power to it hadn't been shut off, and had my sister not been exceptionally careful, could have been badly hurt. The state of the outlet should have caused a fire, and had that outlet been used it definitely would have.

Immediately my sister began crying. There had been no further disturbances in the house since my visit, though they had all remained vigilant of the old woman and their etheric boundaries. As soon as Ellen realized what was happening, she knew the woman had been trying to warn them that the outlet was dangerous. She thanked the spirit profusely for attempting to alert them to the danger, and all has been safely quiet since.

Chapter Fourteen - True Plastic Shamanism

You've read all of my wild stories, some a little creepy, some sweet, but all laced with the supernatural. Do you want to know the scariest thing that has ever happened to me? All things considered, and absolutely hands-down, it was becoming a mother. I don't just mean the addition of offspring into my life, which for me was twins, but all of the mental, psychological, emotional, neurological, chemical—hence physical, and yes, spiritual changes that came with it. In short, through pregnancy and post-partum depression I came to realize just how much neurology and state of mind influence our relationship with the unseen.

One of the first things apparent to me during pregnancy was being cut off from my upper chakras. For those of you who don't know what that change indicates, the upper chakras are considered the spiritual bridges to intuition, the higher aspects of ourselves, and ultimately to our concept of the Divine (Upper World cosmology). Through the upper chakras our higher guidance coaches us, supports us.

I've always had a very open and clear connection to my upper chakras, more so than to my lower chakras. Because of that, I was more prone to journeying to far out spirit worlds, rather than down into the spiritual domain of formed being (Lower World cosmology). It's logical that in pregnancy, most of the emphasis is on the body and its spiritual needs, which are not necessarily the spiritual needs of the mind and psyche. The body endures many physical and spiritual changes to manifest new form, so the emphasis shifts to the mother's lower chakras.

The lower chakras are the energy bridges connecting us into the Earth's life force, into the spirits of Nature and their font of spiritual wisdom and guidance. Emphasis on the lower chakras forced me to be more present, more grounded in the Nature component of spirituality. While beautiful and wonderfully supportive, the change in my etheric focus was debilitating, and it left me quite out of sorts. Imagine being right-handed all of your life, then suddenly being forced to write with your left hand. It's possible, yet challenging enough to impact how you communicate what you know, what you need to express. I could live through my lower chakras. I was still highly intuitive and aware, but a lot of what came in made no sense, as I no longer had access to my higher support system to help me process it.

I recognized this shift for what it was, as it was happening. I quickly discovered that knowing what was happening didn't make finding balance any easier. Pregnancy, itself, is enough to discombobulate, obviously. Still, I can't stress how much that shift in etheric polarities threw off my perception of myself and the worlds around me.

Primarily, it manifest in not being able to hear my guides. I could feel them, and I knew they were with me, but I could no longer journey out to them as I was accustomed. I couldn't engage them in direct support and counsel, after drawing on my bond with them as spiritual sustenance for twenty years. Compound this vertigo-inducing change with the chemical onslaught of paranoia and hypervigilance and the outcome was fairly bleak PTSD. I began to feel that I couldn't trust my own judgment, and I no longer had my guides whispering discernment.

The other significant way this change impacted me was that I couldn't journey out. I'd studied up on how pregnancy would affect me etherically, and I knew that I would eventually reach a point along gestation that it would no longer be safe for me to journey out. It wasn't so much a threat to the babies or to myself from errant energies; rather, it took too much of my energy from caring for them and myself to journey. I was prepared for this change, and accepted it.

However, compounded with not being able to connect with my guides made not being able to journey harder to swallow. I didn't force the issue, though I grieved the lack, and relied heavily upon my practice of mindfulness to keep me present. For this reason, I'd taken hiatus from working with clients several months prior, and didn't resume shamanic work with others until the babies were almost a year old. Such work just wasn't possible or safe at that time.

The evenings were the worst. I sundowned and felt completely paranoid. I'd had all the training someone could have in realizing that these things were merely gaps in my usual perception. I *knew* this intellectually, but my sensual experience told me something other. It said that my atmosphere was hostile, that it was something I should fear, and that I couldn't trust myself or it. I employed mindfulness techniques round the clock, Zen-talking myself from ledges, which I fully credit with any shred of awareness I maintained. Though, combine these nightly episodes with feeling cut off from my guides, and these pockets of darkness were the way post-partum depression manifest for me: a contest between mindfulness and an altered reality of persistent fear.

One experience in particular typified this era of my growth. At around six months old, the kids acquired a toy that I particularly disliked from the moment it was brought into the house. It was a stationary zebra that spun around and bounced, then when turned on, whinnied and played music. The sounds would stop playing after a certain point, effectively switching itself to "sleep" mode—though the literal switch was still set to "on." Still, if the toy was touched or one of its levers moved, it would play again. Taking up residence in the middle of our rec room, the kids loved the zebra. My problem was that it would light up and play music when it had set itself to sleep.

We deduced that if we walked heavily nearby, the toy would come out of sleep mode and play, one time. Never repeatedly, even if you stomped near it, just that one irritating cycle of music. No big.

Then we began to hear it playing in the middle of the night, when obviously no one was near it and there was no movement. Again, just one play cycle. The random animation really started to get on my nerves, to the degree that I researched if it had a sleep timer that played one cycle at interval. Nadda. According to its description, once in sleep mode, the toy is supposed to stay in sleep until touched or switched back on. So, to keep the creepy zebra from randomly playing, we made sure we turned it off when not being used.

But of course the kids were tiny, and we were exhausted. They didn't know how to turn the zebra off, and we often forgot to check it. I'd wake in the night to strains of it playing, imagining its flashing lights dancing on the rec room walls. I didn't personalize its odd behavior, as my lover commented on it playing sometimes when I wasn't home. Fine. But something about it struck me as not quite right.

I kept waking to the zebra playing in the wee hours, which always occurred the same time as when I had panic attacks. Part of my body's return to chemical stasis involved waking around 4am, nightly, in cold sweats and terror. And each time I did, that zebra played, like clockwork.

Animating at that time was one thing. I somewhat got used to it, though it frazzled my already shot nerves. Another factor in the mix was that I had to be up at 5:30, readying for work, and I was the only person up and around, the house completely pitch black that time of year. One morning, after just edging back to sleep from rousing terror and zebra serenade, my alarm went off, and the zebra played a second time.

Again, I was willing to consider it a fluke, until it began to play every morning as I got ready for work. I'd hear it in my 4am reveille, then again as I headed down the stairs, grabbed my lunch from the fridge, or as I walked out the door. The toy wasn't being triggered by movement, and I began to feel that there was life force around it that was trying to tell me something. Whatever it was trying to tell me, my state of heightened vigilance couldn't let me relax and connect with it. I couldn't shift out of paranoid gear.

One night as we readied the kids for bed, the zebra played. Finally thinking straight, I went down to the rec room and turned it off. I could feel that there was something in the room, a presence near the zebra, though not connected directly to it, just nearby, using it, elemental. As I probed, the life force neither clarified its intentions, nor reached back to me. Harmless enough, I fell back to 'no harm, no foul' and left it alone.

A few minutes later, I walked into the hall sporting minty fresh teeth and teapot pajamas, when it played again. As always, when the wyrd starts to be pushy, I go from creeped out to pissed. Whether due to my inability to grok some cryptic spirit memo, or the overzealousness of a needy soul, boundary-violating inundation makes me angry. Well, this time, in my jaded brain soup a combo of fear and rage deluded me. Yet wits intact, I decided to confront the presence.

Entering the room, I left it dark. A few feet into the space, I began my ritual to call in the directions, bringing in the land elders, ancestors, Nature spirits... Right when I got to that part the zebra lit up and started playing.

Apparently somebody didn't need to be called in, as they were already there, and they wanted me to know it. The toy animating despite that it was switched off startled me so badly I screamed and bolted down the hall. I sensed no danger about the situation at all, still the encounter was an abrupt confrontation. My lover and I decided right then and there that it was time to faze out the zebra.

I knew just getting rid of the zebra was no solution to the underlying problem, despite that I had no idea what the problem was. So, hair standing and skin crawling, I went back to the room and finished the ritual, telling the presence as nicely as I could that it needed to find a gentler way to communicate with me because I would no longer respond to theatrics.

The next day, I set out to connect with my guides on the matter. Still a bit chemically murky on trance, I pressed through and entered journey state, calling to my feminine guide, Cailleach. I felt her reaching back to me, though she didn't immediately come. It was the zebra who greeted me by my familiar firelit circle. The same colorful, bouncing plastic toy was as it appeared to my formed eye, only in the Lower World, its life force was vast, commanding. There was nothing at all untoward about its energy or intentions. I realized instantly that it had indeed been trying to tell me something and thanked it for coming to the circle. Cailleach came shortly after, she and I talked about what had been happening. I put my hand on the toy and asked Cailleach to show me its spiritual significance, to show me its message.

What came was a vision of a caregiver from my childhood who often had severe mood swings. In the vision, this caregiver intentionally cast her mood swings into food that was fed to me as a child, the digestion of which into my etheric field was very similar to my experience of post-partum. Essentially, I learned that my caregiver had imparted an imprint of her psychological issues to me, and my postpartum body chemistry was playing them out, over and over. I thanked the zebra, the holder of this healing story, and processed the information with Cailleach.

I had been doing a great deal of healing work on my neurotransmitters, supporting them naturopathically, working with them etherically to bring them back into balance after pregnancy and childbirth. I knew that to heal my mental state, the best I could do was support the body in its experience. And frankly, it had been through a lot. I wasn't expecting an overnight miracle. I couldn't rush it or force my agenda for clear-headedness. Yet nothing that I, other healers, or my doctors did to reboot my biochemistry resulted in healthy improvement. However, once I saw this vision involving the person from my childhood, a fog lifted. I did begin to think more clearly shortly after that journey. The paranoia and hypervigilance abated. I still woke at 4am (every parent does), but I could go right back to sleep. My progression to clarity and a stronger etheric self became within my active grasp.

Despite my all of my efforts to support my wellbeing, without the tapping on the shoulder from the zebra and the manic episodes, I wouldn't have thought to check into that hidden pocket of my childhood experience. I didn't even know it existed. Without learning of that experience, I couldn't heal a part of my etheric mapping that was wounded in my childhood. Until the old wound around chemical imbalance could be addressed, new strides in balancing my neurotransmitters couldn't be made.

The crazy had served a purpose. Self-playing zebra toys are the telephone of the

Universe ringing. That I couldn't answer to interpret the message was the frightening part.

I've never seen the toy's spirit in my soul travels again, and the zebra never played again, unless it was switched on and engaged with the kids. We still have it, only because we keep forgetting to move it out, along with all of the other outgrown toys.

Is my etheric experience of postpartum common, just not widely observed? I don't know. How much of my paranoia was cosmic fine tuning of new maternal instinct? I can't say, but it did hone just that. I do know that I now have nicely balanced intuitive support from my upper and lower chakras, leaving me more intuitively connected than ever. My ability to journey has strengthened, as well, and I do regularly engage in ecstatic trance, though I don't have to, to interact with my guides, anymore. Through the experience of not being able to journey out, my relationships with them internalized in a way that doesn't require me to have to journey. I carry the blueprint of contact with them in me, everywhere I go, now.

And I have two happy, healthy children.

Chapter Fifteen - Seven Things the Dead Want Us to Know About Life

In over forty years of intuitive communion, several universal messages have been conveyed. The unifying concept in these messages is that what happens in consciousness stays in consciousness, and I distilled them to seven general observations:

- *How we live now is the state of the afterlife.* While the body ceases to be, the mind and soul carry on. The state of our consciousness in life is the state of our consciousness in death. If we foster worry and anxiety now, that's our mode of operation after. By focusing on negative or hurtful aspects of life, we stew in them in death, causing consciousness to stagnate. If we are mindful and live in the present in life, in death we continue to broaden consciousness, further opportunity to make choices to support that awareness.

- *There is no magickal place of punishment or reward.* This insight garners strong emotional reactions from many people. Most of our world religions are built on the idea that regardless of the plight of our lives, we are destined by our actions to spend everafter in torment or joy. Again, what the dead indicate is that what comes after is based on our perspective in life. How one behaves in life is what one experiences after life.

- *There is no supreme good or evil.* Source is. As with non-polarized destinations in the afterlife, so is the force of Life, itself. It just is. Neither good, nor bad. Neither ally, nor foe. As Source is in everything, All Things choose how they manifest. We are what we are.

- *Everything lives on.* We are at our base, life force. In some guise, form, or unform, the essence of every thing remains and becomes some other manifestation of itself and All Things.

- *Spirits aren't wise or moral just because they are out of form.* Our culture perpetuates a myth that upon death souls become penitent and/or enlightened. In my experience, wise deceased were so in life. Souls that were confused, frustrated, angry, etc, are so in death.

- *What we don't heal in life stays with us in death.* Thoughts, habits, or beliefs that don't support us or undermine us, such as lying, using others to further ourselves, or denying our true natures do not magickally vanish when we leave form. For this reason, when we seek to release harmful dynamics from our lives, we are also assuring peace in death. We assure ongoing tranquility.

- *Working with trance states affects knowledge of how to die.* By accessing the imagination via ecstatic trance, dreamwork, or other method of altered consciousness, we experience life without the ego. In this pure space and consciousness, we catch glimpses of what it feels like to be out of form, to be our undaunted wild selves. The more we connect with our true nature our quality of life improves. The better we live, the more comfortable we are with the truth of mortality.

While my experiences with the spirits now are more balanced than those of my childhood, the prevailing message is that spirits do affect our lives. By living well we die peacefully, which means that we have no need to disrupt the living. By living well, everyone's experience of consciousness is improved.

Praise for Gift of the Dreamtime

Harrell draws you into the dreamtime as an expert novelist draws you into a great novel and shares with you her experiences and knowledge of the world beyond the veil from the time she was very young. ~ *Innerchange Magazine*

In this book that hunger and fear that nibbled and clawed at you and me for years is explained in poetic, experiential detail. Kelley guides us into our own souls, turning the "whys" into wise. ~ Bridgett Walther, author of *Conquer the Cosmos*

Let S. Kelley Harrell guide you on a very special spiritual journey — destination your healed soul! ~ Donna Henes, author of *The Queen of My Self*

Absolutely recommend *Gift of the Dreamtime* to anyone, especially those working to overcome their own traumas. ~*Facing North*

Kelley Harrell acts as a guide to help us move from deep trauma to wisdom. A brave book, beautifully insightful, that leads us to greater knowing of ourselves. ~ Gail Wood, author of *The Shamanic Witch*

Gift of the Dreamtime gives hope for those of us who sometimes feel we're not doing things right, or that perhaps there is no healing to be had. ~*Pagan Book Reviews*